To the memory of Lucy Sprague Mitchell,
Margaret Wise Brown's teacher—
and mine
—J.W.B.

To my children
Melissa, Ivo & Hilary
—T.B.A.

The Days Before Now

An autobiographical note by Margaret Wise Brown

Adapted by Joan W. Blos

Illustrated by Thomas B. Allen

Simon & Schuster Books for Young Readers
Published by Simon & Schuster
New York London Toronto Sydney Tokyo Singapore

This is to say
that I was born in a brick city
on a wide street of cobblestones.

The street ran down the hill
to the East River
where boats came in
from all over the world
and blew their whistles
and sailed by.
My father made rope
and his docks were at the foot of this street
and there was a smell of hemp in the air
and of rope and tar.

At the other end of the street
was a large brick church
rising into the sky.
And when the doors were open
there was the flash and flicker
of gold and candlelight
and the mystery of stained glass windows.

My mother and father came from
Virginia and Kentucky and Missouri
and I always heard of those places.

Once my great-aunts from Kentucky
who, I had been told, were giants—
they were very tall and beautiful—
arrived in our house for dinner
and I came down in front of the fire to meet them.

They were going across the ocean
on a boat next morning.

That is all I can remember
except the sound of horses' hoofs.
And all this was in one of the many parts
of New York City
before I was four years old.

Then I drove one day in a big open car,
with my grandmother's hat tied on her head
with a big veil blowing

until we stopped.

That was Long Island, and we moved
into a red brick house under some sweetgum trees.

I grew up along the beaches

and in the woods
of Long Island Sound.

This was the country.
And from then on I was terribly busy
hitching up all the dogs I could find
to pull me around on my sled in the snow,

and picking cherries high up in cherry trees,
chasing butterflies, and burning leaves,

and picking up shells on the beach,
and watching new flowers
come up in the woods
as the seasons passed.

I had thirty-six rabbits,

two squirrels—one bit me
and dropped dead—

a collie dog,

and two Peruvian guinea hens,

a Belgian hare,
seven fish,
and a wild robin
who came back every spring.
And all of this happened
in the days before now.

Now I live in a wooden house
in the middle of New York City.
I have written more than sixty books,
and I wish I didn't have ever
to sign my long name
on the cover of a book;
I wish I could write a story
that would seem absolutely as true
as Peter Rabbit and Snow White.

I have a young Kerry blue terrier named Crispin
and a black cat with a big, fluffy tail
named Hyacinth.
My house has a brick floor,
and fireplaces,
and a garden.

Fall leaves fall on it,
winter snow snows in it,
and, in the springtime,
it is full of flowers.

Every summer I go away from my city house.
With Crispin and Hyacinth for company,
I go off into the woods of Maine
to live near the edge of the ocean.
My house in Maine
is called The Only House.
But that is another story.

Afterword

Gifted and charismatic, Margaret Wise Brown (1910-1953) is best remembered for her <u>Goodnight Moon</u>, the bedtime, nighttime, and all-time favorite of generations of children. But she was also the author of many other works (105 published titles, according to one count), several adaptations and translations, a large number of poems and short pieces that appeared in magazines and collections of one kind and another, and a great quantity of unpublished writings.

The text of <u>The Days Before Now</u> is adapted from an autobiographical entry written by Margaret Wise Brown for the second edition of The H.W. Wilson Company's <u>Junior Book of Authors</u>, published in 1951. It is an unconventional little piece, choosing to emphasize the immediacy of childhood while eschewing the usual autobiographical credits and chronologies such as birth date and schooling, parents' names and occupations, marriage and first job. Even in its original form, confined as it was to narrow columns of print, the essay's rhythms are impetuous, its colors bright as Crayolas.

After not having seen it for a number of years, it was my pleasure, in the course of a recent rereading, to realize that this plainly printed note was a picture book waiting to happen! Indeed, so strongly does it imply the genre that finding appropriate line breaks and establishing pagination seemed almost a matter of following instructions implicit in the text. In a very few places, mindful of a young audience, I made the decision to abridge certain lines or to span a passage with a brief improvisation. As none of these changes is substantive, I think that <u>The Days Before Now</u> may fairly be described as vintage Margaret Wise Brown: a piece fully intended for publication by its author and written when her powers were at their incomparable height.

I am enormously grateful to The H.W. Wilson Company, original publishers of this pristine work. Not only has permission been given to free the text from its restrictive format and to make the changes required for conversion to a book for children, but also, by special arrangement, it will be possible to contribute permission fees to the Memorial & Library Association of Westerly, Rhode Island, where they will be used in support of the Margaret Wise Brown Memorial Collection, a valuable resource containing manuscripts, books, and related materials.

I would like to express particular gratitude to Bruce R. Carrick, vice president of The H.W. Wilson Company, whose understandable caution and initial skepticism gave way to gracious approval of the project as a whole.

Joan W. Blos
Ann Arbor, Michigan

Illustrations on pages 30 and 31 were inspired by a Phillipe Halsman photograph
that appeared in the December 2, 1946, issue of *Life* magazine.

SIMON & SCHUSTER BOOKS FOR YOUNG READERS
1230 Avenue of the Americas
New York, New York 10020
The typeface is 18 point Weiss Bold
The illustrations were done in pastel and charcoal.
Manufactured in the United States of America
10 9 8 7 6 5 4 3 2 1

Library of Congress Cataloging-in-Publication Data

Blos, Joan W.
The days before now / an original adaptation by Joan W. Blos of an autobiographical note
by Margaret Wise Brown ; illustrated by Thomas B. Allen.
p. cm.
Summary: The celebrated children's book writer describes the scenes of her childhood,
in New York City and on Long Island, and how she lived as an adult.
1. Brown, Margaret Wise, 1910–1952—Biography—Juvenile literature. 2. Authors,
American—20th century—Biography—Juvenile literature. [1. Brown, Margaret Wise,
1910–1952. 2. Authors, American.] I. Brown, Margaret Wise, 1910–1952.
II. Allen, Thomas B. (Thomas Burt), ill. III. Title.
PS3503.R82184Z59 1993 813′.52—dc20 [B] 93-12814 CIP AC
ISBN: 0-671-79628-3